KURDS

Dr John King

WAYLAND

First published in 1993 by Wayland

Wayland
338 Euston Road
London NW1 3BH

Wayland Australia
Level 17/207 Kent Street
Sydney NSW 2000

Series editor: Paul Mason
Designer: Kudos Editorial and Design Services

This edition
Wayland Commissioning Editor: Jennifer Sanderson
Design: Robert Walster
Editor: Sonya Newland

Acknowledgements:
The artwork on page 5 was supplied by Peter Bull.
The author and publishers would like to thank the
following agencies for allowing these pictures to be
reproduced: Rex Features 4 (David Grahame Baker),
6, 7 (Ozturk), 8 (Jacques Witt), 9 (G Sipalinogh), 11,
12 (Sipa 13 (A Cavalli), 14, 16 (Sipa Press), 25, 26, 27 (J
Schneider), 28 (J R Wilton), 29 (Sipa Press), 30 (Sipa
Press), 31 (A Cavalli), 32 (Aiza), 34, 33 (O'Donnell), 35,
37 (Sipa Press), 38 (Sipa Press), 40 (Kaveh Golestan), 43
(Sipa Press), 44 (T Hall), 45 (A Cavalli); Eye Ubiquitous
10 (J Burke), 19 (J Burke), 20, 21, 22, 23, 24, 36, 41 (JB),
42 (JB); Corbis 18 and cover (P Turnley).

A CIP catalogue record for this book is available from
the British Library.

ISBN 978 0 7502 5579 0

Printed in China

Wayland is a division of Hachette Children's Books,
an Hachette Livre UK company.
www.hachettelivre.co.uk

This book has been produced in consultation with
the Minority Rights Group; an international non-
governmental organization working to secure justice
for ethnic, linguistic, religious and social minorities
worldwide who are suffering discrimination.

Contents

1 Introduction

⬆ An old Kurdish woman, part of a community in the mountains of Kurdistan. The Kurds have lived in the lands that lie on the borders of Turkey, Iran and Iraq for many centuries.

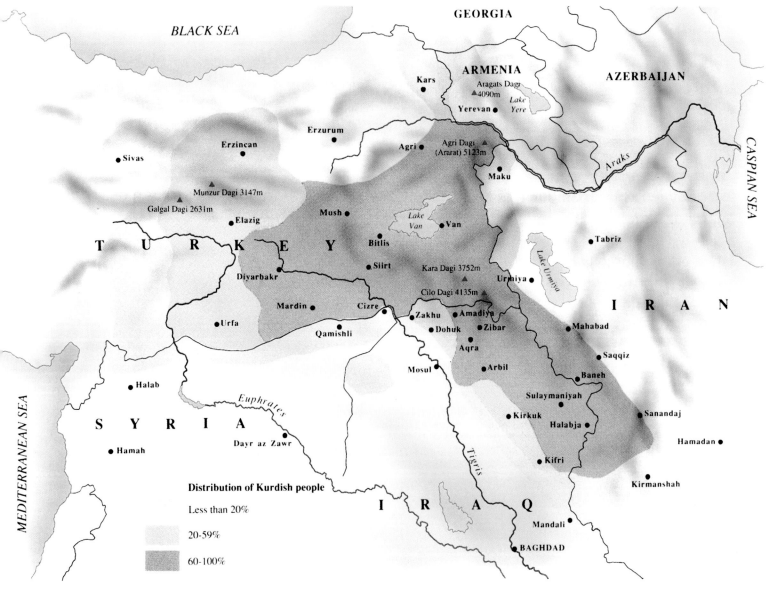

There are at least 30 million Kurds living in the inaccessible mountainous heart of the Middle East, where the Iraqi, Iranian and Turkish borders meet, in a region called Kurdistan. There are also Kurds in Syria, Lebanon, Armenia and Azerbaijan.

Spread of the Kurds

Emigration has spread the Kurds all over the world. There are 500,000 Kurds in Germany and Kurdish communities in other European countries. Kurdish exiles live in London and the Kurdish Institute in Paris promotes Kurdish culture. They can also be found in the USA, Canada and Australia.

The Kurds are unrelated to the Arabs, Turks and Iranians who live around them.

Their language is related to Persian, the language spoken in Iran. They are distantly descended from the Indo-European peoples who moved into the Middle East 4,000 years ago. At that time the Kurds were fierce warriors, and children were brought up to be proud of their traditions. They have retained this pride in their heritage.

The Kurds have their own culture and traditions, and they want their own country. Whether they are able to go on being Kurds, proudly speaking their own language and living their lives in their own way, may depend on whether or not they can get a country of their own. This is because the governments of the countries they live in want them to stop thinking of themselves as Kurds.

2 A Kurdish boy in Iraq

Ziyad lived with his mother and father in the north of Iraq. He called his country Kurdistan. He was born in the town of Arbil. His family had a little house just outside the town, built of brick, with an orchard and some fields. Ziyad helped his mother and father with their sheep and goats, and learned to read and write at the village school. He had an older brother called Massoud, and two little sisters named Hikmat and Nabila.

In 1980, when Ziyad was still a baby, Iraq went to war with Iran. At first the war was far away in the south: the family saw pictures on television of the terrible battles and of the Iranian prisoners of war. There were always pictures of Saddam Hussein, the Iraqi leader, and the Iraqi generals. The television news said Iraq was winning the war. The report was in Arabic, which Ziyad learned at school, but he spoke Kurdish at home.

When the war moved closer, Iraqi soldiers came to the village. The Iraqis thought the Kurds were helping the Iranians. Many of the Kurdish men were arrested and taken

⬆ Kurdish boys in their classroom. Although they are encouraged to think like young Iraqis, Iranians or Turks – instead of Kurds – most of them remain proud of their Kurdish identity.

Attack on Halabja

⬆ The body of a mother and child killed in the Iraqi army's attack on Halabja.

away by the Iraqi police. Then there was a rumour that the Iraqis were taking the people from whole villages. In March 1988, the Kurds of Arbil heard that the Iraqis had done something dreadful at the Kurdish town of Halabja, near the Iranian border. People coming from the east said everybody in the town had been killed with poison gas.

At war with the Iraqis

Ziyad's father explained that the Kurds had been struggling for a long time to have their own country, where they would decide on their own future. The Iraqis had always opposed them. He told Ziyad and Massoud that there were Kurdish fighters called *peshmerga* hiding in the hills, who defied the Iraqis and were ready to die for the freedom of Kurdistan. Massoud said he wanted to join the *peshmerga*. Akram laughed and said Massoud could go when he was older, if they would have him.

In 1991 Iraq went to war again, and this time invaded the rich country of Kuwait, far to the south of Kurdistan. Massoud was 18 years old by this time and had to join the Iraqi army. Ziyad's mother and father cried, but Massoud went off to the south in his Iraqi army uniform. It seemed strange when in fact what Massoud really wanted to do was join the *peshmerga* and fight against the Iraqis.

Ziyad and his sisters never saw their brother again. Massoud went to Kuwait with the Iraqi army. But armies came from the United States and Europe, and Iraq's army was defeated. Massoud was killed when the Iraqi soldiers tried to escape through the desert.

Fighting for freedom

Food was very scarce in the north, and there was no petrol for the lorries that brought supplies to the Kurdish villages. Most of the Iraqi soldiers were at war in the south.

So the *peshmerga* decided it was time to fight for Kurdistan. They came down from the mountains and drove out the Iraqi troops, and then they went into the towns and sent all the policemen and the Iraqi officials away.

For a few weeks the Kurds thought they were going to have their own country. They hoped that the Americans would help them against the Iraqi government. They tore down all the pictures of Saddam Hussein and put up pictures of their own leaders, Massoud Barzani and Jalal Talabani. But the Americans did not help them, and after a few weeks the Iraqi soldiers came back. They had powerful guns and tanks, and the *peshmerga* were driven from the places they had captured only a few weeks before.

Fleeing to the mountains

The people were very frightened of what the Iraqi soldiers might do: many Kurds went with the *peshmerga* up into the mountains by the Turkish border. Ziyad's family also went. At first they travelled in a lorry with some other families. Then they had to walk. It was very cold, and the little children got very tired. Eventually they camped at the

⬆ The wreckage of Iraqi trucks and tanks that tried to escape from Kuwait after the Iraqi invasion in 1991. Many Kurds were forced to join the Iraqi army and died in the invasion.

↑ Kurdish guerrillas in a mountain stronghold. Guerrillas have been fighting for many years in the hope of setting up an independent Kurdistan.

top of a hill. Some people were ill and died, especially old people, babies and small children. People from European countries such as France and Britain came and gave the family tents and food, and foreign doctors came to help the people who were ill.

Because the Americans and British had not sent an army, just a few soldiers to help protect the Kurds, everyone was still very frightened of what the Iraqis might do. To save the Kurds from attack by the Iraqis, the Americans agreed to fly their planes from their bases in Turkey over the Kurdish lands.

A time of hope
Eventually Ziyad's father decided it was safe to go home, so they made the long journey back to Arbil. The Iraqi soldiers had gone and

were camped to the south: they were afraid of the foreign planes that flew overhead. The planes would attack the Iraqi soldiers if they came into the Kurdish country.

In 1992 the Kurds held an election to decide who should lead them. Ziyad was fourteen, almost a man, and he was very excited on election day, riding up and down with his friends in a truck covered in posters of Barzani, the Kurdish leader Ziyad's family supported. Everyone thought that the Kurds might now get their own country of Kurdistan at last. But the Kurds had been disappointed before.

Ziyad thought that if the Kurds still had to fight for their own country, he would go to the hills and fight for the *peshmerga* as Massoud had wanted to. His parents were very proud of him.

3 A Kurdish woman in Iran

In her village in Iran, near the town of Mahabad and not far from the frontier with Turkey, Shireen was about to be married. She was 17 years old. She lived at home with her mother and two sisters. Her older sister Jahan was already married and had a child, but she and her husband lived in the family home. Jahan's husband helped to support the family, because Shireen and Jahan's father was away working in Mahabad. Their father sent money home, but Jahan's husband did the work on the farm.

Life on the farm

Shireen's family kept sheep and goats, and farmed a plot of land. Their house was made of mud bricks, with doors and window frames painted blue. In the dusty courtyard were

⬆ Kurdish refugees who fled from the Iraqi army at the end of the Gulf War in 1991. Iran gave many Iraqi Kurds shelter.

⬆ A Kurdish mother and her daughters shelter from the hot sun.
Many Kurds in Iran live on small farms like this.

pumps to bring up water and old petrol cans to carry it into the house. In the winter it got very cold at night, and the family huddled near the warm bread oven.

Shireen was getting married to Jalaluddin, who worked in a shop mending television sets in Mahabad. That was where he had met Shireen's father, who brought him home to visit. Jalaluddin had his school leaving certificate and was well educated. He wanted to go to Tehran to work, or even abroad. Shireen had never been to school. Lessons were difficult because they were in Persian, which was different from the

Kurdish the family spoke at home. And her mother needed her to help about the house.

Rule from Iran

The old men used to tell tales about how the Kurds had once had a country of their own with a government in Mahabad, for a short time after the Second World War (1939–45). But that was long ago, before Shireen was born, and after a year the Shah had sent his army and stopped it. The Kurds were again governed from Tehran, the Iranian capital.

Shireen's father said that some of the people thought it might be better for the

A woman in Iran wearing a black *chador*, a cloth cover for her hair and clothes. The Kurds who live in Iran must fit in with the Muslim government's ideas.

Kurds when the Shah was overthrown and driven out of Tehran in 1979. Soon, though, Ayatollah Khomeini's troops put the Iranians in charge again.

There were groups of men in hiding in the hills who wanted a separate Kurdistan in Iran, but most of the Kurdish people just wanted to live peacefully. When Iran was fighting Iraq, Shireen would hear the planes, and there were terrible stories about what happened to the Kurds across the border in Iraq.

Future hopes

In 1991, when the Kurds in Iraq were trying to get away from the Iraqi soldiers, thousands of refugees came across the border. Shireen wondered if some of them might be her cousins, and whether she and her family could do anything to help, but they didn't have much money and it was hard to know what to do.

Shireen was unsure what the future might bring. But she knew Jalaluddin was a good man and she hoped she would be happy. She was not certain how much she cared whether the Kurds had a country of their own, but she did not much like the Iranian soldiers.

A young Kurdish girl

'Pushing her small sister ahead of her, Zeynep prods at the geese to drive them back into the yard. She knows how to look after babies and has two younger sisters to attend to. Now she stands with her hands on her hips, imitating her mother, and bellows at Ozlem to walk in front of her and keep the geese under control. One day a man's family will come to see her father and will bargain with all the elders to fix her bride price, and then she will be decked with gold bracelets, earrings and necklaces, new dresses and new shoes, to fulfil her role as a Kurdish female in her community.'
(Sheri Laizer, *Into Kurdistan*, Zed Books, 1991)

4 A Kurdish man in Turkey

Mehmet was 20, and lived in Kars, a town in eastern Turkey where many people were Kurdish. He was a taxi driver: he often waited by the bus station for people who came from other towns. He liked to talk to them, especially if they were Kurdish.

When Mehmet finished work he liked to go to one of the tea-houses near the bus station. Only men were out at night, and in the cafés they played games such as backgammon and dominoes. Kurdish musicians played in the tea-house. Until recently, the singers were not allowed by the government to sing in Kurdish, but everybody knew that in spite of the Turkish language they were Kurdish singers and the songs were Kurdish.

When Mehmet finished paying for his taxi, he hoped that before he was too old he

⬆ Men at a café in Turkey, passing the time with games and coffee. Kurds sometimes go to cafés to hear recordings of Kurdish singers.

13

might have enough money to get married. He had a cousin who lived in Germany and worked in a factory in Düsseldorf. Mehmet wondered if he should go to Europe to try to earn his fortune. Some people made enough money in Germany to come home and buy a farm. Then their relatives could live in comfort and work on the farm while they went back to Germany to work again.

The PKK

In south-eastern Turkey, where Mehmet originally came from, his family was poor. His father and uncle were dead. And there was trouble, because the men from the Kurdish Workers Party, the PKK, sometimes

⬆ Turkish troops in Kurdistan. The military have fought the Kurdish PKK for more than two decades.

came at night and attacked the police and soldiers. Then the police were hard on all the Kurds. Boys Mehmet had known at school had gone to the mountains to join the PKK, and he didn't want them to come to any harm.

Second-class citizens

Mehmet understood what made the PKK angry. The Turks refused to let the Kurds speak their own language, except between themselves. They made the Kurds feel like second-class people. The Turks had always been against letting the Kurds have their freedom, unless they agreed to abandon their own traditions and become Turkish in their ways like the rest of the population in the area. And there was a tough military government in the south-east of Turkey where most Kurds lived. The young people felt they had no future unless they could have an equal chance at life in a country of their own.

5 History and politics

The Kurds are descended from Indo-European tribes who moved into the region they now call Kurdistan around 4,000 years ago. The Kurds are mentioned by an ancient Greek author, Xenophon, writing in around 400 BCE, who says that a Greek army met some people called the Kardukhoi on the borders of Persia. Xenophon wrote that the Kurds of his day were very warlike, and defied the Persian emperor.

Conversion to Islam
When the Arabs brought the Islamic religion to the region in the seventh century CE, the Kurds resisted the new religion and fought against the invading Arabs. But the Arabs won a great battle near the modern Iraqi city of Suleymaniyah in CE 643. The Kurds converted to Islam, but kept their political independence on the borders between the Arab, Persian and Byzantine empires for many centuries. Despite this, though, there was never really a unified state of Kurdistan, and the Kurds relied on the difficult mountain country and on the distance between them and the Arab, Turkish and Persian armies to keep them safe from their powerful neighbours.

During the Crusades the Kurds, whose fighting men were fierce warriors, made their

Dates in Kurdish history

11 July 1880 Sheikh Ubaidullah writes to British consul in eastern Turkey setting out national claims of the Kurds.

23 July 1908 'Young Turks' take power in Ottoman Empire, and recognize some Kurdish rights.

10 August 1920 Treaty of Sevres (recognizes Kurdistan).

24 July 1923 Treaty of Lausanne (divides Kurdistan between Iraq and Turkey).

5 March 1926 Frontier treaty between Turkey and Iraq, giving the Kurdish area north of Mosul to Baghdad.

16 October 1945 Iraq crushes Kurdish revolt.

15 November 1961 Beginning of Kurdish revolt in Iraq led by Mustafa Barzani.

29 June 1966 Iraqi government claims Mustafa Barzani has accepted a peace plan.

11 March 1970 Iraq offers Kurds autonomy, but is rejected.

23 September 1974 Iraq claims total victory over Kurds.

6 March 1975 Iraq and Iran sign frontier agreement. Iran withdraws help for Iraqi Kurds.

12 September 1980 Turkish military coup followed by mass arrests of Kurds.

22 September 1980 Iran-Iraq war begins.

15 August 1984 First PKK attacks in Turkey.

17 March 1988 Iraqis massacre Kurds at Halabja.

2 August 1990 Iraq invades Kuwait.

13 April 1991 US President Bush says he will not become involved in any civil war in Iraq.

19 May 1992 Kurdish parliament elected in northern Iraq.

15 February 1999 PKK leader Abdallah Öcalan captured.

April 2002 Turkish government legalizes broadcasts and education in the Kurdish language

20 March 2003 US-led forces invade Iraq.

30 January 2005 Kurdish party alliance comes second in Iraqi elections.

16 December 2007 Turkey launches air strikes on Kurdish PKK fighters in Iraq.

29 February 2008 Turkey withdraws from Iraq.

influence felt widely in the territory that is Syria, Lebanon and Israel today. The famous Muslim hero Saladin (Salah aI-Din Yusuf), born in CE 1138, was a Kurd.

After a battle at Lake Van in 1514 between Persia and the Ottoman Empire, most of the Kurds came under Ottoman rule, but they kept much local independence.

Turkish rule

The Ottoman Empire was broken up at the end of the First World War, in 1918. Britain and France, who were among the victors,

Kurds in Lebanon

There are thought to be around 80,000 Kurds living in Lebanon today, although exact numbers are not known. They are not considered to be very important in Lebanon. Their identity cards do not give them full Lebanese citizenship, even if their families have lived in the country for generations.

The difficult treatment the Kurds have had to endure in Lebanon made them sympathetic to the left-wing PKK. Lebanese Kurds, and Kurds from elsewhere in the world, attend the guerrilla training camp known as the Mahsum Korkmaz Military Academy. This was set up by the PKK in Lebanon's Bekaa Valley, an area of Lebanon controlled by Syria. In 1992 Turkey asked Syria to stop guerrilla training there, and put pressure on its Arab neighbours to bring it to an end. Despite this, the academy continued to attract new recruits and its graduate numbers increased in the mid-2000s.

⬆ Kurdish *peshmerga* guerrillas. The word *peshmerga* means 'one who faces death'.

agreed in 1920 to set up an independent Kurdistan. This was to be in part of the territory of modern Turkey and Iraq. However, the new Turkish leader, Kemal Ataturk, persuaded Britain and France that they should let him found a Turkish state. The Kurds were disappointed, but at first Ataturk said it would be a state for the Turks and Kurds to share equally. In fact, Ataturk incorporated Kurdistan into modern Turkey, ruled by Turks. The original treaty was forgotten.

In 1923 the Treaty of Lausanne divided Kurdistan between the different modern states of the Middle East. Most Kurds found themselves living in Turkey: they are the ancestors of the 14 million Turkish Kurds of today. Another large group was in Iraq, which became fully independent in 1932. Other Kurds found themselves living in Iran, as well as Armenia and Azerbaijan, which were part of the Soviet Union until 1991.

Forced to fit in

The Kurds did not forget their desire for a country of their own, and this began to clash with the ideas of the states in which they were living. Iraq is intended to be a state for Arabs, in which the language and culture are Arabic. Turkey is a state for the Turks, where Turkish is spoken and Turkish ideas control what happens. Iran is an Islamic republic, where Kurdish culture has to come second to Islamic beliefs and traditions. It is hard for the Kurds to fit into these backgrounds.

The Kurds have not ceased to struggle against the governments of the countries in which they live. There were clashes between the Kurds and the governments in the years in between the two World Wars. In 1974, Iraq offered the Kurds an agreement on autonomy, but talks broke down and in a short and brutal war thousands of Kurds died. In Iran, clashes between Kurds and the Iranian army led to the killing of thousands of Kurds from 1980 to 1984. Hostilities between the Kurds and the Iranian government continued into the twenty-first century. In Turkey there has never really been peace between the Kurds and the Turkish authorities. In 2002 the European Union succeeded in making the Turkish government reinstate some Kurdish rights. However, the Turks continued to mount military operations against the PKK.

The Kurds have never stopped fighting for an independent state, and in recent years they have come to believe that their culture will not survive if they do not achieve a separate political status.

Kurdish nationalist movements

IRAQ

KDP (Kurdish Democratic Party)
Founded by Mustafa Barzani in 1946. Current leader Massoud Barzani.

PUK (Patriotic Union of Kurdistan)
Split from KDP in 1975. Leader Jalal Talabani.

Kurdistan Islamic Union
Founded in 1994. Leader Salaheddine Bahaaeddin.

IRAN

PDKI (Kurdish Democratic Party of Iran)
Founded 1945. Leader Mustafa Hijri.

Komala
A pro-communist front founded in the early 1940s. Leader Abdollah Mohtadi.

TURKEY

PKK (Kurdistan Workers' Party)
Founded 1974 by Abdallah Öcalan. Current leader Muray Karayilan. Party also known as KADEK.

DTP (Democratic Society Party)
Founded 2005. Considered by some to be the political wing of the PKK.

6 Who are the Kurds?

A family in Turkish Kurdistan at a farm near Lake Van. Kurdish families are often large, because the people expect their children will support them when they are older.

Most Kurds live in Turkey. There are around 14 million Kurds there, out of a population of more than 70 million – an estimated 20 per cent. Then there are over five million in Iran, between four and six million in Iraq, perhaps up to 2.8 million Kurds in Syria, more than half a million in Azerbaijan and Afghanistan, and over a million elsewhere, including about 80,000 in Lebanon.

Kurds in Iraq

The Kurds who live in Iraq suffered badly at the hands of Saddam Hussein during his time as leader (1979–2003). In 1991 many of them fled their homes, into the mountains up by the Turkish border. The world's sympathy was aroused as news programmes were filled with stories of the hardships the Kurds faced, and pictures of families living in freezing conditions in tents, or tiny children and old people carrying heavy loads.

Kurds in Turkey

The Turkish Kurds have suffered a long history of repression by the Turkish government. Kurds believed they were denied their rights as citizens, because they were not allowed to use their language, and because they believed the Turks hated them and discriminated against them. In 2002, the Turkish government legalized broadcasts and education in the Kurdish language, but they were still denied many other freedoms.

Kurds in Iran

In Iran the Kurds are treated more fairly, but they have to put the demands of religion before their own Kurdish identity. This is because Iran has a religious government.

Shared traditions

Whatever country they live in, all Kurds have a lot in common. They all speak Kurdish, and they recognize the language of other Kurdish speakers. There are several different dialects, depending on which part of Kurdistan a person comes from. The main ones are Kurmanji in the north and Sorani in the south. The Kurds are aware of the separateness of their language, which owes nothing to their Turkish and Arab neighbours. Their shared language, and the traditions, tribal stories and folk tales that go with it, are things every Kurd is proud of. Men and women can tell the stories their fathers and mothers passed down to them.

Religion

Another thing many Kurds have in common is their religion: most are Sunni Muslims. Many Kurds also belong to Sufi religious brotherhoods. This means they meet to chant and dance together to worship God, as well as saying their ordinary prayers. These brotherhoods are very important to the Kurds.

Although most of the Kurds are Sunnis, about one-fifth of them are Shi'ite Muslims, like the Iranians, including most of those who live in Iran. Others belong to various sects, such as the million or so Alevis in Turkey and the smaller group of Yezidis – an unusual religion that has taken features from different faiths. Many Yezidis live in Armenia and Azerbaijan. A few other Kurds belong to smaller Muslim sects. There are also a few Christians living among the Kurds, who speak Kurdish like their neighbours and are sometimes regarded as Kurds. But it is not religion that makes the Kurds different from their neighbours: most of the people in the countries around them are also Muslims, after all.

United by history

What makes a Kurd regard himself or herself as a Kurd is mainly the language, and the long, shared history of common experience – often characterized by trouble and persecution. The Kurds believe they all come from a common ancestry and are proud of themselves and the way they are able to live in their inhospitable but beautiful mountain environment. They are also very conscious of their shared traditions and their ancient warrior past.

Many ordinary Kurdish men and women would like to live quiet lives with their families. But they are caught up in the changing politics of the regions where they live. Though many Kurds in Turkey, Iraq and Iran take little interest in politics, they cannot ignore the political changes that are constantly taking place around them.

Political changes

Although Kurds in Iraq have been more free to use their own language and practise their own traditions than they have in other places, government repression has still been harsh. Kurds have their own parliament and something like a homeland of their own, but they are still fighting for recognition of their own independent culture. As war raged

⬅ An armed Kurdish man in Zakho, in northern Iraq, with his daughter. Even when caring for their families Kurdish fighters in northern Iraq carry their weapons.

⊕ These Kurdish refugees in northern Iraq live in a damaged army truck.
A whole way of life in the Kurdish villages has been destroyed.

between Iraq and US-led international forces, a 'safe haven' was created for the Kurds in the north. Despite this, the Kurds face an uncertain future there.

In Turkey, ordinary Kurds in the south-east of the country hear every day about the battles between the Kurdish militants of the PKK and the Turks, and every Kurd knows someone who has been killed. The Turkish government continues to fight the militants, and has mounted incursions into northern Iraq.

In Iran, the Kurds face the harsh rules of the Islamic Republic, and some of them wonder if the chance will ever come to have a separate country. After the Second World War an independent republic was established around the Kurdish city of Mahabad in Iran, but this collapsed after only a year.

So all Kurds, wherever they live, know that they are different from the rulers of the country their villages and towns are part of. The Kurds are also aware that across the borders are other people who feel the same, and who tell the same stories about their past.

The Kurds know that in the past the tribes used to wander from one part of their lands to another. They never had to submit to the Turks or the Persians. They still tell stories about Kurdish heroes, and about the Kurdish chiefs who at one time or another ruled part of Kurdistan. Some of the greatest figures of the Muslim world have been Kurdish.

7 Kurdish life

Traditional Kurds mainly live off the land, but they farm in different ways. Some live in the high mountains, where they keep herds of goats and flocks of sheep. Others live in villages in the valleys or down on the plains, where they are farmers. The men and women share the work in the farms and the fields, and the boys and girls help from a young age.

There are also Kurdish towns. In Turkey, Diyarbakir and Van are Kurdish towns, and Diyarbakir is almost like a capital city for the Kurds. In Iraq, the Kurds live in Arbil and Kirkuk as well as in other towns in the north. In Iran, Mahabad is the main Kurdish town.

Traditional dress

The Kurds today dress in much the same way as their Turkish, Arab and Iranian neighbours. In Turkey the men wear mainly Western clothes. In Iraq they add woollen coats and waistcoats, chequered scarves wrapped round their heads like turbans, and sometimes baggy trousers. The women wear a Muslim style of dress, often also with baggy trousers, sometimes under layers of skirts, and they often choose bright colours. But some women dress more like women in the West. The women sometimes cover their heads in the Muslim way, especially in Iran, where the Islamic Republic prefers women to wear a *chador* (see page 12).

➲ Traditionally, Kurdish women wear brightly coloured dresses and scarves around their heads.

Clothes

'There are two kinds of traditional Kurdish clothes – one for men and one for women. The women's dresses are different colours and have beautiful patterns on. They are long. The men's clothes are made of nice material – they are trousers and a top and we have a long piece of material that we tie round our waist. Men also wear a hat. If we go to a Kurdish party we wear Kurdish clothes.'
Hazan Shoresh, aged 11 (*Voices from Kurdistan*, Minority Rights Group, 1991)

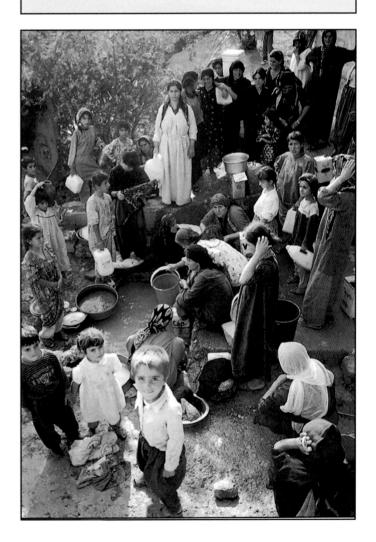

● A Kurdish man wearing traditional baggy trousers herds his sheep. Sheep-herding is one of the only types of farming possible in the high mountains of Kurdistan.

There is a traditional style of dress that is gradually dying out, where the men wear baggy trousers and waistcoats and the women wear their brightly coloured skirts. Some Kurds still wear at least part of the traditional costume though.

Employment

In the Kurdish villages of Iraq and Turkey, many villagers still work at farming and traditional crafts. But their apparently peaceful way of life has been increasingly disrupted in the past two decades by the effects of political clashes, especially with the Ba'athist government of Iraq, and with the government of Turkey.

The Kurds are herders, and goats and sheep are an important part of village life. The flocks and herds provide milk and meat, and sometimes products such as leather and goats' cheese can be sold. The women make things to sell, such as carpets, while the men look after the livestock. Flocks and herds are the chief livelihood of the mountain Kurds, some of whom are nomadic. The Kurds grow fruit and vegetables to eat, and the villagers who live on the lower slopes or on the plains also grow wheat to make flour for bread. Some Kurds grow tobacco to sell, mainly in the local towns. In Turkey, Kurdish farmers grow cotton that they sell. But most Kurds farm to feed themselves, not to make money.

The women make cloth and rugs, and some Kurdish men are expert at repairing the trucks they depend on to travel between villages and to the towns. A few villagers work as merchants, and others as blacksmiths or builders.

In villages on the lower slopes of the hills, and especially in the towns, the Kurds do many different kinds of work. They are shopkeepers, carpenters, plumbers, teachers and bank managers. Because of their unsettled lives and their uncertain future, many young Kurds are looking to a future outside Kurdistan, and perhaps even abroad. In Iraq, it is difficult for the Kurds to leave their own areas, and it would be unpleasant for them to live outside the Kurdish region. In Turkey, many young Kurdish men work in the towns. If they succeed there, they sometimes come home to find a Kurdish girl to marry, and then bring up a family away from Kurdistan. Few Kurds marry people who are not also Kurdish.

Some young men and women move abroad to work: there are as many as half a million Kurds in Germany. There are also

⬆ Some Kurds work as traders in the towns, like these men selling wool in Van, Turkey.

⬆ Kurdish children in school. They are normally taught in the language of the country in which they live, even though they are used to speaking Kurdish at home.

Kurds in the Netherlands and in other places in Europe. Some Kurds go abroad to get away from the police in Turkey, Iraq or Iran. Kurds who live away from Kurdistan often send money home to help their relations who have stayed behind.

Language

In both Iraq and Turkey, the Kurds are encouraged to regard themselves as Iraqis or as Turks, and to abandon their separate Kurdish identity. In Turkey, printing books or performing songs in Kurdish was banned until 1991, for example. In parts of Iraq Kurdish traditions are still not encouraged.

If Kurdish children go to school, they normally have their lessons in Arabic or Turkish, even if the teachers are Kurdish. The radio and television broadcasts they hear and see are in Arabic, Turkish or Persian, depending on where they live. Although this helps the Kurdish children to learn foreign languages, it is not good that they never hear Kurdish spoken outside their homes. If no one around you speaks your language, you may start to feel that it is useless.

Of course, having lessons in a foreign language makes it difficult for Kurdish children to get the best out of their schools. Even when they can understand what their teachers are saying, it can still be difficult for them to do their homework and they often perform badly in written examinations.

Religion and politics

The Kurds who live in the mountains often still regard themselves as members of different tribes. That means that they see themselves as related to other families who live near them, in a stronger tie than just being neighbours.

In the old days, a village or local leader known as the *agha* was often important in village life. The *aghas* still play a part, but their influence is not so strong now. Young Kurds in particular listen to the Kurdish politicians and the militant movements, and make up their own minds on what to think and do rather than asking the older men as they might have in the past.

Sufi brotherhoods (see page 20) are popular with the Kurds. The leaders of these

brotherhoods (called *shaikhs*) often still have a good deal of influence over the other members of the brotherhood.

Today more people listen to the Kurdish political parties, the Patriotic Union of Kurdistan and the Kurdish Democratic

← There is not much work for the older men in Kurdish villages in Turkey. These two men pass the time in conversation.

Kurdish demonstrators in Berlin call for peace in Turkish Kurdistan. There are around half a million Kurds in Germany.

Party in Iraq, and in Turkey the revolutionary movement known as the PKK (see page 32).

The political difficulties the Kurds are facing mean that it is hard for them to keep their traditional way of life unchanged. Many Kurds in Iraq have had to move from their homes, both because of deportations enforced by the Iraqi government and because they fled from Iraqi troops after the Gulf War in 1991. Despite some moves towards greater tolerance, in Turkey there is still conflict between the Kurds and the Turkish army and police. This grew worse when the PKK began its attacks on the security forces in 1984. The situation in Turkey is complicated by the rejection by some Kurds of the PKK's communist ideas: this does not necessarily mean that they do not want an independent Kurdistan. Other Kurds have moved to different parts of the country and adapted to Turkish life.

8 Problems today – Iran

The first modern Kurdish nationalist was Shaikh Ubaidullah, who launched a revolt against the Shah of Persia (now Iran) in 1880. The shaikh tried to set up an independent Kurdish state, free of both Persia and the Ottoman Empire.

In 1919, another famous Kurdish shaikh, Mahmoud Berezendji, took control of the Suleymaniyah region of Iraq from the British troops who had moved into Iraq at the end of the First World War. Shaikh Berezendji, who called himself the King of Kurdistan, also had influence in Iran: in 1923 he fled there from the British.

During the Second World War, Mustafa Barzani led another widespread nationalist uprising. Mustafa Barzani was the father of one of today's Kurdish leaders, Massoud Barzani. At the end of the Second World War, in 1946, the Kurds briefly had a state of their own in part of western Iran, with its capital at Mahabad. The Shah of Iran tolerated the new Kurdish state for less than a year, until he was able to send troops to crush the rebellion against him. Barzani fled north to the Soviet Union.

Since then there has been little effective agitation for independence on the Iranian side of the border. Both before and after the Islamic Revolution, the Iranian authorities have kept the Kurds under close surveillance and control.

Muslim unity

In the early 1980s the Iranian government thought of giving the Kurds some independence. But the plans did not go far enough for Kurdish leaders, and fighting began again. Some of the Iranian Kurds are Sunni Muslims like their cousins across the border in Iraq and Turkey. The religion of Iran is Shi'ite Islam, but the Iranian leader at the time, Ayatollah Khomeini, said that as far as he was concerned there was no

⬅ General Mulla Mustafa Barzani, a Kurdish hero of the past. The picture was taken in 1946, when General Barzani became President of the Kurdish Republic of Mahabad, which lasted only a year.

⬆ Iraqi soldiers at the front in the war between Iran and Iraq (1980–88). The Kurds backed Iran in the war.

difference between Muslims who spoke different languages. He meant that although Sunni and Shi'ite Muslims have some differing ideas about their religion, they are all still Muslims and therefore should be able to live together.

Muslim communities

'There is no difference between Muslims who speak different languages. It is very probable that such problems have been created by those who do not wish the Muslim communities to be united. They create the issues of nationalism, of pan-Iranianism, pan-Turkism, which are contrary to Islamic doctrines.'
(Ayatollah Khomeini, former Iranian ruler)

No Iranian government has ever wanted to lose any of its territory. There seems little chance that the Kurds could become independent from Iran with the agreement of the government. Tehran firmly crushed the Kurdish movement inside Iran itself in 1983, but hostilities continued into the twenty-first century.

Border disputes

The border between Iran and Iraq has always been a cause of conflict between the two countries. There have been constant border disputes: from 1980 to 1988 there was a bitter war between Iraq and Iran. The Iranian government has always offered limited help and encouragement to the

↑ Members of the Democratic Party of Iranian Kurds (PDKI). The PDKI leader, Abderrahman Ghassemlou, was murdered in 1989.

Kurds in Iraq. This is mainly a way of annoying the Iraqi government. In 1991, after the Gulf War, the Kurds rose against Saddam Hussein. Soon after, many thousands of Kurds crossed the border to Iran because they feared revenge attacks. The Iranian authorities opened the border and behaved generously to the Kurds, but probably only because they could later be used against Iran's enemy Iraq.

Iran's policy to the Kurds always has Iran's own interests in mind, and the government in Tehran would not allow the Kurds today to act against the Iranian state. The assassinations of Kurdish officials who were visiting Germany in September 1992 seem likely to have been the work of the Iranian secret service. The murdered men

belonged to the Kurdish Democratic Party of Iran (KDPI), which was founded during the Mahabad Republic.

Kurds in Iran today have learned that the government insists they must regard themselves simply as citizens of the western part of the country. Though the government is prepared to recognize them as a religious minority and allow some of them to practise Sunni Islam, and though the use of their language is not forbidden, they still have no separate status.

If a Kurd is prepared to regard himself or herself as an Iranian citizen, life in Iran is easier. Kurds occupy many government posts, but Tehran still appoints police chiefs and other key officials, and all Kurds feel as if they are living under supervision.

9 Problems today – Turkey

The struggle between Turkey's Kurds and the Turkish government goes back a long way. After Turkey was made an independent state under Kemal Ataturk in 1924, he banned the Kurdish language, clothes and all public activity by Kurds. He wanted to make the Kurds into Turks. Ataturk wanted a Turkish state, and he would not tolerate people who wanted to be different. The Turks even began to claim there were no such people as Kurds, only what they called 'mountain Turks'.

The Kurds rejected Ataturk's plan for them to become Turks, with their usual attitude of proud independence. There were terrible battles between the Kurdish people and the Turkish authorities in the east of Turkey in the 1920s and 1930s. Whole villages were destroyed, and people were moved away from their homes. Many thousands died in the fighting.

The Kurds were defeated, but never forgot their separate heritage. Over the years there has been quiet resistance by the Kurds, who in private have always used their own language and kept up their old customs.

Forced to forget the past

Politically, the aim of all Turkish governments since Ataturk has been to make the Kurds forget their past and become Turks. That is, to make them a part of the nation, so that there would be no difference between Kurds and Turks. But the Kurds have never accepted this policy. The Kurds have long memories, and know that if

◑ Even ordinary villagers in Turkey have become used to harsh treatment from the police and the army. This has led many young Kurds to support the PKK.

Ataturk had kept his word, they would have had a homeland of their own in south-east Turkey.

For a while after the Second World War, life was easier for the Kurds. There was a free election in 1950, and the Turkish Democratic Party won it. They allowed exiled Kurds to return home, and gave property back to those from whom the government had taken it as a punishment. A new constitution in 1961 even allowed the Kurds to express their own ideas and have their own organizations, so long as they used the Turkish language.

But in 1967 the government of Suleiman Demirel again began to clamp down on the Kurds. (Suleiman Demirel was re-elected as prime minister of Turkey in 1992.) The government was determined to keep a close control of south-eastern Turkey, because it bordered Iraq, Iran and the Soviet Union, and because oil resources were discovered there. The military regime that held power in 1980 clamped down on the Kurds even more tightly, and the army ruled Turkey until 1983.

The PKK

Because they were allowed less and less freedom to be Kurdish, the Kurds once again began to fight against the government. In Diyarbakir in 1967, there were the biggest anti-government demonstrations since the 1930s. And an important development in the 1970s was that a Kurdish leader called Abdallah Öcalan formed the group known as the PKK, or Kurdish Workers Party. The PKK is organized as a political party, but it also has a tough military wing. Since 1984, PKK groups have attacked the Turkish army and police in Kurdistan, and continue to do so. Not all Kurds approve of the PKK, because their attacks often bring trouble to the Kurdish villagers. The Kurdish villagers are mostly against the Turkish government, but they often do not like the communist ideas of the PKK. The PKK says that it would control the economy and agriculture.

Women in the PKK

'The party has always attached great importance to the struggle of women for freedom and spared no effort in this direction. This struggle of ours has resulted in the mass participation of women in the revolution, and in women actively taking their place in society. Women are involved both in the uprisings and in the guerrilla struggle. There are now more than a thousand women guerrillas, and the number is increasing daily.'
(Abdallah Öcalan, in *Kurdistan Report*, 1992)

The PKK was an offshoot of a group formed by Kurds at Ankara University in 1974, which aimed to get recognition for Kurdish language and culture. The PKK was more radical, with a mixture of nationalist and Marxist ideas. It was led by Öcalan until his capture in 1999. When they started military action in the 1980s, PKK groups were allowed by the Syrian government to use bases in Syria, and set up a guerrilla training camp in Lebanon.

The PKK attacked police and army posts in Turkish Kurdistan. The group's first aim is to establish a Kurdish state in Turkey. Eventually it would like to see a bigger

PKK guerrillas

'At the camp known as the Mahsum Korkmaz Academy, [named after a PKK member who died in a battle in Turkey] I found hundreds of people in well-cut olive drab military fatigues, much more disciplined and military in aspect than any of the local militias. Hearing English spoken, I soon found myself talking with Milan, an olive-skinned teenager who had come from Australia, where her Kurdish parents had gone for work. Now she was a soldier in the war against Turkey. "I am trying to forget I ever knew English", she said. "All I care about now is Kurdistan."

('Confrontation in Kurdistan', Christopher Hitchens, National Geographic, August 1992)

⬆ PKK guerrillas in their camp in the mountains of Kurdistan, preparing for an operation against the Turkish army.

Kurdistan in territory taken from Turkey, Iraq, Iran and even Syria. The PKK demands help and support from Kurdish villagers inside Turkey. Villagers who object have been attacked and sometimes killed. In Turkish villages the police search ruthlessly to try to root out PKK militants, so they base themselves outside Turkey and slip over the borders to carry out their raids. The PKK is absolutely forbidden inside Turkey, but it has many supporters, especially among young Kurds. South-eastern Turkey is very poor, and many of the young people do not see any future for themselves within Turkey. They believe that their only chance for change is to break free from Turkish control.

Throughout the 1990s and the early 2000s, increasing numbers of ordinary Kurds in Turkey secretly began to support the PKK. Even moderate Kurds believed that the PKK was their only hope for the future. A moderate Kurdish leader, Mehdi Zana, a former Mayor of Diyarbakir, said the PKK was the only national Kurdish movement in Turkey, and that the people should support it. In the 1990s the Turkish government tried to compromise with the Kurds. It announced that the Kurdish language would no longer be banned. This did not go far enough for most Kurds, because though it was no longer a crime to speak Kurdish in public, there were still no Kurdish newspapers and no Kurdish radio or television. In 2002, when Turkey was trying to join the European Union, Kurdish broadcasts were finally allowed.

Militant activities

But permitting Kurdish broadcasts did not mean that the Turkish government was any less tough in its campaign against Kurdish militants. Turkish intelligence agents attacked people they suspected of being Kurdish militants. There were also more casualties in clashes between government forces and PKK guerrillas. Thousands of people have died in these clashes since the 1990s. When the PKK leader Öcalan was captured in 1999, the group's activities slowed down for some time. However, in 2004 the campaigns began again.

Party politics

Within Turkish Kurdistan, the Kurds are largely controlled by Turkish police officers and Turkish troops. Kurds vote for local representatives but these representatives form part of the Turkish political system, rather

● For many years, Kurds in Turkey had read the news in Turkish, because it was against the law to print newspapers in the Kurdish language.

than a Kurdish one. The Kurdish Democratic Society holds a number of seats in the government, but because it is believed to be linked to the PKK, it is viewed warily by the Turks and many international governments.

The struggle between the Turkish security forces and the PKK involved both Turkey's neighbouring Arab countries and the Kurdish movements across the frontiers. Syria allowed the PKK to operate from its territory. In 1992 the Turks asked Syria to stop encouraging this and to prevent the PKK training guerrilla soldiers in the Lebanese camp, in territory controlled by Syria. Despite these calls for cross-border support to halt the training of Kurdish militants, the PKK has continued to operate.

Meanwhile the main Kurdish movements in Iraq began to try to prevent the PKK from crossing the frontier into Iraq. The Iraqi

Kurds have their own struggle with the Iraqi government, and they do not want to antagonize the Turkish government. In 1992, the Iraqi Kurds helped the Turkish army to drive the PKK out of northern Iraq to stop them attacking Turkish targets from across the border.

The Turkish government wanted to be seen as modern and liberal. This was partly because of its desire to join the European Union (then the European Community), so it wanted to appear as an orderly state. But at the same time it was still using force to kill or capture PKK members and those who supported Kurdish nationalism.

Forced assimilation

Many Kurds, just like most other people, want to live quietly and to be allowed to try to make their living as best they can. Kurds who are proud of their cultural heritage sometimes reject the methods of the PKK. But at the same time they resent the way the government does not recognize them as a separate people.

Some Kurds have moved to non-Kurdish parts of Turkey, to try to escape police persecution. They try to live like other Turks, at least in the eyes of their neighbours and the authorities. If enough Kurds act in this way, the Kurdish way of life could one day disappear altogether. Meanwhile other Kurds avoid persecution entirely by emigrating, mostly to Europe. Germany is the most popular destination, with around half a million Kurds living in communities there.

← Iraqi *peshmerga*, which clashed with the Turkish Kurds of the PKK, who were using camps in northern Iraq to launch attacks across the border into Turkey.

⬆ A patrol of Turkish troops takes PKK members prisoner. The Turks (in white snow uniforms), have been scouring the high mountains for Kurdish *peshmergas* trying to evade capture.

Kurds in Turkey

'The young boy stood by his picturesque village on the edge of Lake Van and expressed the quiet Kurdish determination that seems sure to confound Turkey's new tendency towards a military solution to eight years of separatist insurgency. "I want a Kurdish state, a Kurdish flag, red, yellow and green," he said, as if repeating a basic creed. "I don't want the Turkish flag any more." Why? Was he not grateful for the neat Turkish health clinic standing on the edge of the village? The only explanation the boy had was the one that can be heard all over the south-east of Turkey: a Kurdish consciousness has been awakened, a fact that Turkey has refused to accept seriously after decades of denying the Kurdish identity.'
('The Kurdish nationalist genie', Hugh Pope, *Independent*, 6 October 1992)

It is hard to say that the Turkish government has modified its old policy of trying to assimilate the Kurds. On the other hand, it is equally hard to see if that policy can ever be fully achieved. The Kurdish population is so large and determined not to become part of the larger state that however hard Turkey tries, it may never be able to absorb the Kurds.

If the Kurds cannot get a state in their own part of Turkey, and Turkey will not abandon its repression of the Kurds, perhaps the best hope for the future is that Turkey may eventually come to accept the possibility of some kind of federal state. This would recognize the Kurdish identity of the south-western part of the country. Otherwise, Kurdish culture seems doomed to face continuing Turkish repression and persecution.

There are somewhere between four and six million Kurds in Iraq. It is here that the Kurds have been persecuted by the government to the greatest extent. But it is also in Iraq that the Kurds have come closest to their aim of setting up a separate Kurdish state.

Uprising in Iraq

At the end of the Gulf War, in February 1991, Allied forces led by the USA drove Iraq's army from Kuwait. It seemed that getting rid of President Saddam Hussein was among the USA's war aims. Some of then-US President Bush's statements could have been understood this way. Militant groups among the Kurdish population of northern Iraq rose up against Saddam Hussein and his government in Baghdad.

The rebels saw that the Iraqi state was in a weakened condition at the end of the Gulf War. They thought they would be able to overthrow Iraq's authority in the northern Kurdish part of the country and set up their own state. They also believed that they would get some help from the victorious USA. In fact, the USA refused to provide Iraqi rebels with the help and support they hoped for.

The result of the failed Kurdish uprising in the north of Iraq was that much of the civilian population fled into the inaccessible mountains of northern and eastern Kurdistan. The refugees then attempted to cross the borders into Turkey and Iran. Iran admitted refugees, but television pictures of the Turkish border showed men, women and children living in appalling conditions in makeshift homes in the mountains, without

🔄 Kurdish guerrillas after the uprising at the end of the Gulf War.

Kurdish women in Iraq

'The women's union in the city of Suleymaniya is housed in what was an Iraqi Ba'ath Party Office before the Kurdish uprising. Here Sirwar Rasheed, the headmistress at a girls' school in Suleymaniyah, explained the problems Kurdish women face today in the urban environment. In one room of the building women were running a sewing workshop making childrens, clothes to sell in the market. Like many others, Sirwar has not received her teaching salary for months. She continues to teach but has not been paid. Like their rural counterparts, many middle class Kurdish women like Sirwar are also struggling to make ends meet.'
(Julian Gearing, 'The Ones Left Behind', *The Middle East,* December 1992)

enough food and medical care. The Turkish government would not allow many Kurds across the border. International aid agencies tried to help the Kurds in their mountain camps, while the Kurds hoped desperately to be allowed into Turkey.

Some Western troops were moved into Kurdistan to help protect the population. The initiative that helped the Kurds most was a US decision to seek United Nations backing for an air exclusion zone. This meant that Iraqi planes were forbidden to fly north of a specific line. The area north of this line included much of Iraqi Kurdistan. US planes based in Turkey patrolled the sky to make sure the rule was obeyed.

In the safety this protection gave, the Kurds organized elections in 1992 for a Kurdish government, even though Iraqi troops were waiting just beyond the southern border of the Kurdish region. The Kurds established a parliament in northern Iraq, and were able to govern this area without too much interference from the Iraqis.

⬆ The smaller man in the red and white scarf at the centre of the picture is the Kurdish Democratic Party (KDP) leader, Massoud Barzani.

War against the government

The two main Iraqi Kurdish organizations had most of the seats in the Kurdish parliament and most of the posts in the new Kurdish government. These two movements were – and still are – the Kurdish Democratic Party led by Massoud Barzani, and the Patriotic Union of Kurdistan led by Jalal Talabani. These parties organized a meeting of other Iraqi opposition groups, and together they planned resistance to Saddam Hussein in other parts of the country. When US forces invaded Iraq in 2003, and a new war broke out, Kurds assisted in fighting the Iraqis. The Kurds suffered many casualities in the war.

The resistance to Saddam Hussein at the start of the twenty-first century was just the latest episode in a long history of confrontation between the Kurds and Iraqi governments, dating from the end of the Second World War. In 1970 the then-Iraqi President Bakr proposed a peace agreement that recognized the separateness of the Kurds and accepted the idea of a self-governing Kurdish region. This never really worked, and when fighting began again, there was a short but fierce battle between the Kurds and the Iraqi army. In 1979, the Iraqi Kurds thought they might get some help from the new Islamic government in Iran. During the war between Iran and Iraq, Kurdish armed groups fought against Iraqi

Kurdish children in Iraq

'Everywhere, it seems, there are groups of women struggling to bring up children on their own. Behind typical Kurdish smiles and laughter exist conditions of extreme hardship. Take the case of Merina, a woman living in the rubble of Baroshke village. Merina talked quietly of the loss of her husband and the terrifying exodus that took place at the end of the Gulf War. Merina fled with her children over the cold, muddy mountains to Turkey. She did not want to talk about her youngest daughter. The cold had killed her. She was just three years old.'

(Julian Gearing, 'The Ones Left Behind', *The Middle East*, December 1992.)

forces in the north of the country. Iraq responded with attacks on the Kurds. Many Kurds were forced to move from their villages near the Iranian border, and young Kurds were conscripted into the armed forces and moved away to other parts of the country. Iraq also attacked civilians in Kurdish areas.

The upheavals had a terrible effect on the lives of many women. In the closing months of the war between Iraq and Iran, the Iraqi government split up families and destroyed villages, fearing that the Kurds would help Iran's army. Many men disappeared, and were never seen again. More were killed in the attempt at an uprising against Iraq after the Gulf War. Women were left trying to bring up children on their own, sometimes in dreadful conditions. Today, women are often

⬆ These Kurdish women and their children are living in a makeshift camp, having fled their homes.

⬆ Kurdish *peshmergas* in northern Iraq patrol for signs of an Iraqi attack.

harshly treated by the Iraqis, especially if their men have been killed, and many have to live with terrible memories of maltreatment and cruelty.

For many years the Kurds in northern Iraq have lived against a background of disturbance and political upheaval. Most of the people want to live quietly, but have been constantly harassed by the Iraqi government. Many people think their best chance of a quiet life would be in an independent state or region of some kind. That is why the Kurdish nationalists are so popular in northern Iraq.

In the same way that the Kurds in Turkey have been forced to act as if they were Turks, Kurds in Iraq have only really been able to take part in the life of the country if they regard themselves as Iraqi citizens and use the Arabic language. The situation looked set to improve after an alliance of Kurdish parties came second in a landmark election in 2005, and the PUK leader, Jalal Talibani, was appointed interim prime minister, and later president. No Kurd has ever risen to such a position of responsibility in Iraq.

Though the Kurdish language is not forbidden, education in Iraq is in Arabic, government services work in Arabic, and the television and radio are in Arabic. Because language is so important to the Kurdish identity, the Kurds have always felt like strangers in Iraq. However, recent changes in Iraq have given Kurds hope for the future.

11 The future

Whether or not Kurdish culture will survive depends on whether they can gain independent political status – free from the rule of the countries in which they currently live. The Arabs, Turks and Iranians do not want Kurdish culture to be part of their countries, so the Kurds must have a country of their own. The survival of the Kurds as a separate people is therefore connected to the establishment of the country of Kurdistan.

Kurdistan

Long ago, the Kurds were able to govern themselves, although they were not fully united, and Kurdish chieftains and tribal leaders enjoyed independence in their inaccessible mountain strongholds. Since they came under the domination of their neighbours, though, they have looked back to this time and longed for the freedom they once had. In all the years since, they have kept their sense of cultural identity. Even though the Kurds in the different parts of geographical Kurdistan differ in their outlook and experience, all Kurds feel a strong sense of solidarity.

Kurdistan is a name that has often been used in this book: for centuries it has been used to describe the geographical region where the Kurds live. But it is also the name that Kurds everywhere give to the independent state or country they one day hope to have. They hope this will be a place where they can live and govern themselves,

⬅ This Kurdish woman is ready to fight alongside her PKK colleagues for Kurdish freedom in Turkey.

↥ Despite hardship, the Kurdish spirit is hard to break, and the Kurds are as determined as ever to have political independence.

and where their own culture, traditions and language can be practised.

The country of Kurdistan would not necessarily have to cover the whole area in which Kurds currently live – that mountainous region with land in Iraq, Iran and Turkey. The Kurds just want an area that they can call their own. However, this would mean one or more of the neighbouring countries giving up some of their land to the Kurds, and none of them is willing to do so.

What has become of the three young Kurds we read about at the beginning of this book? Ziyad, the boy in Iraq, did not in the end go to fight the Iraqi army. Iraq's Kurds now have an autonomous region, and Ziyad did not share the fate of his older brother. He and other Kurds of his generation still put up with continued threats from Iraq, though.

Shireen, in western Iran, now lives with her husband Jalaluddin in Mahabad. The Kurds are just one of many different kinds of people in Iran, and the government is not trying to make them exactly the same as other Iranians. But the Islamic government has strong religious ideas about how people should behave, and Shireen has to fit in with these.

Mehmet continues to drive his taxi in Kars, in western Turkey. Perhaps one day he will have his own taxi business. But he will always know that the Turkish police are watching for signs of the Kurds organizing themselves. He will hear stories about raids made by the PKK on army posts or police stations. And he will go to Kurdish cafés to hear the songs by Kurdish singers that are only just being allowed to be heard in

Turkey. Or perhaps he will go to Germany, where he will lead a different life with different problems.

The Kurds have had many years to become used to living in a world where they have no country. Today, they fear that if they do not soon have a part of the world to call their own, their children and grandchildren will no longer be Kurdish, but will be assimilated into the countries where they live. A proud history will disappear, and the young Kurds will have been forced to become Iraqis, Turks or Iranians.

The Kurds are not the only people who do not have a country of their own, but it is tragic that the Kurds have suffered so much, and that for many of them it may continue.

Kurdish nationalism

'Kurdish nationalism, a cause blithely overlooked by the international community for at least a century, is now being brought forcibly to the attention of the West. By its own actions, it is now obliged to take up the cause of the Kurds and reluctantly decide the fate of Iraq as a country. By giving the Kurdish resistance the impression that it had American backing for a renewed uprising, letting it down when it took action, and then intervening in response to worldwide horror at the fate of Kurdish refugees, President Bush raised the intractable question of how the United States would like to see the Middle East rearranged.'
('Kurds: what sort of new order?', in *The Middle East*, May 1991)

⬆ A Kurdish woman and her son face an uncertain future. Much will depend on international help.

Glossary

Agha An agha is a tribal leader (see entry for tribe).

Alevi The Alevis are a Muslim sect found among the Kurds, related to the Shi'ites.

Ataturk Kemal Ataturk was a Turkish nationalist born in 1881. He came to power when he founded the modern state of Turkey in 1921. He died in 1938.

Autonomy Autonomy is the right of a people to govern themselves, possibly within a larger political unit. Autonomy is usually seen as a step short of independence.

Backgammon A board game with dice and counters much played in the Middle East.

Byzantine Empire A Christian state that made up the eastern half of the Roman Empire. It was Byzantium, now Istanbul.

Chador A *chador* is the black veil worn over women's clothes in Iran.

Crusades Religious wars launched by the Christians of Europe against the Muslims in the twelfth and thirteenth centuries.

Exclusion zone A military exclusion zone is an area where hostile aircraft or ships are not allowed to go. The USA declared an air exclusion zone in Iraq in 1991 to keep Iraqi aircraft from attacking the Kurds.

Gulf War The war between Iraq and an alliance led by the United States and Saudi Arabia, was caused by the Iraqi invasion of Kuwait on 2 August 1990.

Iranian The people of Iran are called Iranians. This country was formerly known in the West as Persia, and its language is known in the West as Persian. In this book we have used the word Persian for the language and Iranian for the people of Iran.

National identity A people's national identity means their consciousness of belonging to the same nation, which they think has a right to independence.

Nationalist A Nationalist is someone who feels a national identity (see entry).

Nomadic Nomadic people, or nomads, are people who regularly move with their livestock to better pastures.

Persian *see* Iranian.

Peshmerga A Kurdish guerrilla fighter. The word means 'one who faces death'.

Shah Before the Islamic Revolution in 1979 the Iranian leader was known as the Shah.

Shaikh A *shaikh* is a tribal or religious leader.

Shi'ites Shi'ites are Muslims who follow the faction who believed that Muhammad's son-in-law Ali should have been his successor. Over the years the Shi'ites have developed different religious ideas from Sunni Muslims. Shi'ites tend to rely more on the guidance of religious leaders than do Sunni Muslims.

Statehood Statehood is what a people are said to have when they have achieved a government and a territory of their own.

Sunnis The majority of Muslims in the world are Sunnis, who believe that the leadership of the faith was correctly handed down after Muhammad's death, and have developed a body of religious law by which they believe Muslims should be guided.

Further reading

Kurds in Britain, Cath Senker, Franklin Watts, 2005

The Kurds: A People in Search of Their Homeland, Kevin McKeirnan, St Martin's Press, 2006

The Kurds in Iraq: Past, Present and Future, Kerim Yieldiz, Pluto Press, 2007

Further information

MRG's Education Project produces learning material and information for teachers covering many aspects of minority rights. For more information contact:

Minority Rights Group International
379 Brixton Road
London SW9 7DE
www.minorityrights.org

Survival International is a worldwide movement to support tribal peoples. It stands for their rights to decide their own future and helps them protect their land, environment and way of life. Membership of Young Survival costs very little. When you join you get a newsletter with a Young Survival pull-out page and the chance to buy T-shirts, games, tapes and other Survival goods.

Survival International
310 Edgware Road
London W2 1DY
www.survival-international.org

Index

Numbers in bold refer to pictures as well as text